Notes • Re
to keep my body an

Date:

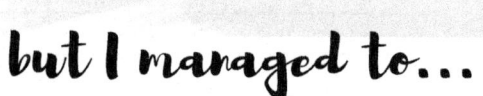

Today I struggled with...

but I managed to...

Notes • Reminders • Ideas
to keep my body and mind healthy and happy

Date:

Today I struggled with...

but I managed to...

Notes • Reminders • Ideas
to keep my body and mind healthy and happy

Date:

Today I struggled with...

but I managed to...

Notes • Reminders • Ideas
to keep my body and mind healthy and happy

Date:

Today I struggled with...

but I managed to...

Notes • Reminders • Ideas
to keep my body and mind healthy and happy

Date:

Today I struggled with...

but I managed to...

Notes • Reminders • Ideas
to keep my body and mind healthy and happy

Date:

Today I struggled with...

but I managed to...

Notes • Reminders • Ideas
to keep my body and mind healthy and happy

Date:

Today I struggled with...

but I managed to...

Notes • Reminders • Ideas
to keep my body and mind healthy and happy

Date:

Today I struggled with...

but I managed to...

Notes • Reminders • Ideas
to keep my body and mind healthy and happy

Date:

Today I struggled with...

but I managed to...

Notes • Reminders • Ideas
to keep my body and mind healthy and happy

Date:

Today I struggled with...

but I managed to...

Notes • Reminders • Ideas
to keep my body and mind healthy and happy

Date:

Today I struggled with...

but I managed to...

Notes • Reminders • Ideas
to keep my body and mind healthy and happy

Date:

Today I struggled with...

but I managed to...

Notes • Reminders • Ideas
to keep my body and mind healthy and happy

Date:

Today I struggled with...

but I managed to...

Notes • Reminders • Ideas
to keep my body and mind healthy and happy

Date:

Today I struggled with...

but I managed to...

Notes • Reminders • Ideas
to keep my body and mind healthy and happy

Date:

Today I struggled with...

but I managed to...

Notes • Reminders • Ideas
to keep my body and mind healthy and happy

Date:

Today I struggled with...

but I managed to...

Notes • Reminders • Ideas
to keep my body and mind healthy and happy

Date:

Today I struggled with...

but I managed to...

Notes • Reminders • Ideas
to keep my body and mind healthy and happy

Date:

Today I struggled with...

but I managed to...

Notes • Reminders • Ideas
to keep my body and mind healthy and happy

Date:

Today I struggled with...

but I managed to...

Notes • Reminders • Ideas
to keep my body and mind healthy and happy

Date:

Today I struggled with...

but I managed to...

Notes • Reminders • Ideas
to keep my body and mind healthy and happy

Date:

Today I struggled with...

but I managed to...

Notes • Reminders • Ideas
to keep my body and mind healthy and happy

Date:

Today I struggled with...

but I managed to...

Notes • Reminders • Ideas
to keep my body and mind healthy and happy

Date:

Today I struggled with...

but I managed to...

Notes • Reminders • Ideas
to keep my body and mind healthy and happy

Date:

Today I struggled with...

but I managed to...

Notes • Reminders • Ideas
to keep my body and mind healthy and happy

Date:

Today I struggled with...

but I managed to...

Notes • Reminders • Ideas
to keep my body and mind healthy and happy

Date:

Today I struggled with...

but I managed to...

Notes • Reminders • Ideas
to keep my body and mind healthy and happy

Date:

Today I struggled with...

but I managed to...

Notes • Reminders • Ideas
to keep my body and mind healthy and happy

Date:

Today I struggled with...

but I managed to...

Notes • Reminders • Ideas
to keep my body and mind healthy and happy

Date:

Today I struggled with...

but I managed to...

Notes • Reminders • Ideas
to keep my body and mind healthy and happy

Date:

Today I struggled with...

but I managed to...

Notes • Reminders • Ideas
to keep my body and mind healthy and happy

Date:

Today I struggled with...

but I managed to...

Notes • Reminders • Ideas
to keep my body and mind healthy and happy

Date:

Today I struggled with...

but I managed to...

Notes • Reminders • Ideas
to keep my body and mind healthy and happy

Date:

Today I struggled with...

but I managed to...

Notes • Reminders • Ideas
to keep my body and mind healthy and happy

Date:

Today I struggled with...

but I managed to...

Notes • Reminders • Ideas
to keep my body and mind healthy and happy

Date:

Today I struggled with...

but I managed to...

Notes • Reminders • Ideas
to keep my body and mind healthy and happy

Date:

Today I struggled with...

but I managed to...

Notes • Reminders • Ideas
to keep my body and mind healthy and happy

Date:

Today I struggled with...

but I managed to...

Notes • Reminders • Ideas
to keep my body and mind healthy and happy

Date:

Today I struggled with...

but I managed to...

Notes • Reminders • Ideas
to keep my body and mind healthy and happy

Date:

Today I struggled with...

but I managed to...

Notes • Reminders • Ideas
to keep my body and mind healthy and happy

Date:

Today I struggled with...

but I managed to...

Notes • Reminders • Ideas
to keep my body and mind healthy and happy

Date:

Today I struggled with...

but I managed to...

Notes • Reminders • Ideas
to keep my body and mind healthy and happy

Date:

Today I struggled with...

but I managed to...

Notes • Reminders • Ideas
to keep my body and mind healthy and happy

Date:

Today I struggled with...

but I managed to...

Notes • Reminders • Ideas
to keep my body and mind healthy and happy

Date:

Today I struggled with...

but I managed to...

Notes • Reminders • Ideas
to keep my body and mind healthy and happy

Date:

Today I struggled with...

but I managed to...

Notes • Reminders • Ideas
to keep my body and mind healthy and happy

Date:

Today I struggled with...

but I managed to...

Notes · Reminders · Ideas
to keep my body and mind healthy and happy

Date:

Today I struggled with...

but I managed to...

Notes • Reminders • Ideas
to keep my body and mind healthy and happy

Date:

Today I struggled with...

but I managed to...

Notes • Reminders • Ideas
to keep my body and mind healthy and happy

Date:

Today I struggled with...

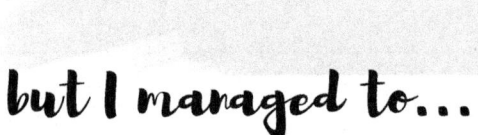

but I managed to...

Notes • Reminders • Ideas
to keep my body and mind healthy and happy

Date:

Today I struggled with...

but I managed to...

Notes • Reminders • Ideas
to keep my body and mind healthy and happy

Date:

Today I struggled with...

but I managed to...

Notes • Reminders • Ideas
to keep my body and mind healthy and happy

Printed in Great Britain
by Amazon